Raspberry Pi
*Beginners Guide to Your
First Project*

DAVID CHANG

Legal & Disclaimer

The content and information contained in this book have been compiled from sources deemed reliable, and it is accurate to the best of the Author's knowledge, information, and belief. However, the Author cannot guarantee its accuracy and validity and cannot be held liable for any errors and/or omissions. Further, changes are periodically made to this book as and when needed. Where appropriate and/or necessary, you must consult a professional (including but not limited to your doctor, attorney, financial advisor or such other professional advisor) before using any of the suggested remedies, techniques, or information in this book.

Upon using the contents and information contained in this book, you agree to hold harmless the Author from and against any damages, costs, and expenses, including any legal fees potentially resulting from the application of any of the information provided by this book. This disclaimer applies to any loss, damages or injury caused by the use and application, whether directly or indirectly, of any advice or information presented, whether for breach of contract, tort, negligence, personal injury, criminal intent, or under any other cause of action.

ISBN-10: 1548722448
ISBN-13: 978-1548722449

CONTENTS

What is Raspberry Pi:

The Raspberry Pi is a cheap single board computer that exposes pins and ports for physical computing. This means that you can attach a wide variety of electronic components to it and drive them from software.

Raspberry Pi

Raspberry Pi primarily runs a version of the Linux operating system called Raspbian but other operating systems can also be used to host software applications that you write. Designed and distributed as a cheap device for the purpose of educating in the skills of computer programming, Raspberry Pi is without question more than powerful enough for a wide variety of projects:

- Science experiences
- Playing games
- Build a robot
- Play music

And a lot of other uses due to its assets such as:

- Small size
- Portability
- cost
- connectivity
- Programmability

Put simply, the Raspberry Pi is a great computer with lot of resources made up to be used and enjoyed by all technology-geek categories.

Setting Up Raspberry Pi

To use and work on your Raspberry Pi, you will need some extra components. Here we are going to show and explain every one of them.

a. The micro SD card:

The first thing we need is an SD card that contains the OS (operating system) of our Raspberry Pi.

After installing the OS, we just put the SD card in the slot and power the Pi.

b. The power supply:

Now we need to power our single board computer with its charger as shown in the image below

PS: power should be around 5V/2A.

c. The USB and HDMI Inputs/outputs:

Once done, and to exploit our computer, we obviously need a mouse, a keyboard and also a monitor.

d. Other ports:

In Raspberry Pi, there are more features that we can explore such as: Ethernet for internet access, Jack input/output for voice and RCA Video output.

Finally, we are able to fully use our mini-board computer.

Pi Product Models

Like any product in the market place, especially technological one, where development and creating new models faster, stronger and better is normal. We should assume that the Pi devices will evolve many models released over the years.

These models have changed their specifications on number of CPU cores, RAM sizes, number of USB ports and headers exposed.

The following is a quick summary of the different models and how they have changed over time:

Model	SoC	Speed	RAM	USB	GPIO
Pi 1 Model A	BCM2835 / ARMv6	700MHz	256MB	1	26
Pi 1 Model B	BCM2835 / ARMv6	700MHz	512MB	2	26
Pi 1 Model A+	BCM2835 / ARMv6	700MHz	256MB	1	40
Pi 1 Model B+	BCM2835 / ARMv6	700MHz	512MB	4	40
Pi 2 Model B	BCM2836 / ARMv7	4 x 900MHz	1GB	4	40
Pi 3	BCM2837 / ARMv8	4 x 1.2GHZ	1GB	4	40
Pi Zero	BCM2835 / ARMv6	1GHz	512MB	1	40

To clarify differences between models we need to explain each criterion of our comparaison:

- SoC (System on Chip): is a microchip with all the necessary electronic circuits and parts for a given system, such as a smartphone or wearable computer, on a single integrated circuit (IC).

- Speed: is the speed of communication between the processor and the other components printed on the Pi.

- RAM (Random Access Memory): is the place in the Pi where the operating system (OS), application programs and data in current use are kept so they can be quickly reached by the device's processor.

- USB (Universal Serial Bus): is a port of communication with external components.

- GPIO (General Purpose Input/Output): are pins of the Pi for mastering and managing other components via pins.

The Pi is composed of a variety of sub-systems that, when combined, provide what we know of as the Raspberry Pi.

- The ARM CPU:

The heart of any computer is the Central Processing Unit (CPU). Within the Pi, the CPU is the ARMv6 or the ARMv7 (Pi 2). ARM Cortex-A7 architecture. This naming can become confusing.

The clock speed on the Pi has a default value but can be overclocked to make it run faster. Before you merrily
increase the speed of your Pi "just because you can", pause a moment. If it were just fine for the Pi to run faster than

its default speed, wouldn't the vendors already have enabled that higher speed? After all, there is no merit in
artificially slowing a processor. The reason that the processor doesn't run at the higher speed is that there is a tradeoff between execution speed and life expectancy of the device.

 If you over-clock it, you are running it faster than it was intended to run under normal operations.

My suggestion to you is to remain at the default clock speed unless you absolutely must go faster … and even then, consult the latest forum posts and other sources of knowledge to read about the negative effects running at the faster speed may cause.

Within your own software, as you start to do development, you may need to compile or build differently depending on the architecture of the machine. You can dynamically determine the architecture of the Pi on which you are running with the command "uname -m" that you can type in the Raspberry Pi **terminal.**

- Broadcom System on a Chip:

The Broadcom BCM2708 is a family of system on a chip devices of which we care about the BCM2835, BCM2836 and BCM2837. These chips provide hardware support for timers, I/O controllers, GPIO, USB, I2C, SPI and UART.
The core reference document for the device is the PDF document called "Broadcom – BCM2835 ARM Peripherals".

When you first obtain a Pi, chances are high that it won't come with any pre-supplied software. As such your first task will be to select an operating system and install it on a micro SD card. I suggest working with Raspbian.

In order to install the Raspbian software we will proceed with the following steps

Step 1: Download the Required Software and Files

At the beginning, you need to download the OS from the following link https://www.raspberrypi.org/downloads/raspbian/

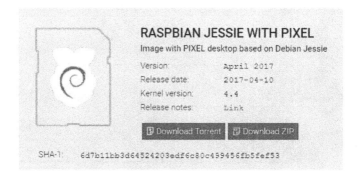

Then you download the SD Card Formatter software
https://www.sdcard.org/downloads/formatter_4/

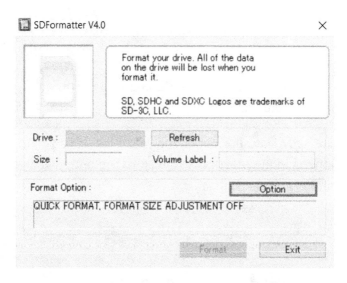

Finally, you will need the win32diskimager software to install the OS on the memory card
https://sourceforge.net/projects/win32diskimager/

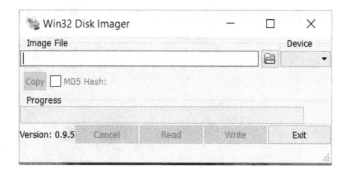

Step 2: Prepare the SD card

Get a minimum 8 GB SD card with a card reader. Insert that card into the card reader and plug that to the USB port.

Go to my computer or my PC and find the drive name where the SD card is **mounted.**

Open SD Card Formatter and select the drive you noticed in the previously, then click on option and put Format size adjustment ON

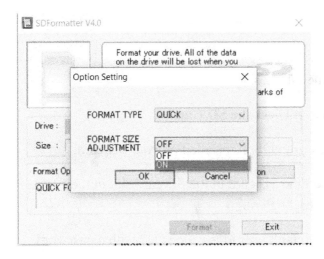

finally click on format

When formatting is completed, click on OK.

Step 3: Write the OS on the SD Card

Open the win32DiskImager software.

Browse the img file of Raspbian OS that was extracted from the downloaded file at the beginning.

Click on open and then click on Write.

Wait for the write to be completed and it may take some minutes. So be patient.

Step 4: Eject the SD Card

Now your OS in installed on your SD card.

Insert the SD card in the SD card slot in the Pi and power the Pi on.

The default user id is called "pi" with a password "raspberry".

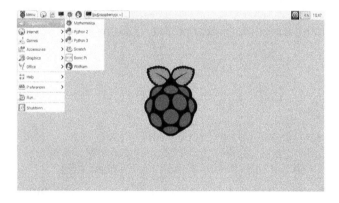

Presentation of the Linux environment: Raspbian

You are now running a Linux environment with all the pros and

cons associated with that.

We notice a clear interface with the desktop and some icons, but to handle a raspberry, we need to learn the basic commands. At the beginning, we have to open the Terminal where we will type command linux.

One of the earliest things you will want to do is run the Raspbian configuration tool, So you type in the terminal: **sudo raspi-config**

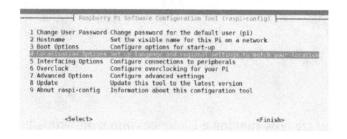

You can change the configurations of your raspberry pi of this interface for example by typing "Location options" you can make the setting of time, language and localization.

To type Select or Finish you use the tab key.

Installation tools

When we think of a Linux operating system, we will find that the state of a system is governed by the existence and versions of files on the file system. If we consider a "package" to be a collection of files necessary to perform some discrete operation, then we can also think of the files on the Linux file system as being members of some package or another (with the obvious exception of application files that you create).

If we wish to install a package, we must obtain a copy of all the files associated with that package and place them in the correct directories where they are expected to be found. If we were attempt to do this by hand, we would end up in all sorts of troubles. Not least of which would be the potentially of making mistakes with manual copies. In addition, some packages are not self contained but instead have prerequisites which are themselves packages.

What we need is some registry mechanism where we can learn what packages are installed and a repository where packages can be found and downloaded. This is exactly what the apt technology does for us.

Next we will look at some of the primary commands for working with packages. The most important of these is **apt-get** We will be using apt-get extensively to install new packages that aren't present in a default distribution.

- **apt-file**

The apt-file tool allows one to find which package might contain a specific file. Note that **apt-file** needs to be installed with the following command:

$ sudo apt-get install apt-file

Once installed, we need to run

$ apt-file update

to retrieve the database of packages and the files

they contains.

To find which package contains a file:

$ apt-file search <filename>

To list files contained in a package:

$ apt-file list <packagename>

- **apt-get**

The apt-get command is a command line interface to the Advanced Packaging Tool (APT) library. It is by far the

most commonly used of the package management tools. To install a package we can run:

$ sudo apt-get install <pkgname>

To un-install a package run:

$ sudo apt-get purge <pkgname>

To download the package without installing it run:

$ apt-get download <pkgname>

The downloaded package will end in ".deb". We can then install that package using"

$ sudo dpkg --install <fileName.deb>

- **apt**

To see which packages are installed, run

$ apt --installed list

Updating

After having installed Raspbian, you will wish to update it to the latest maintenance level. You will also want to perform this task periodically to ensure you have the latest.

To determine the level of the kernel installed, run:

$ uname -a

Linux raspberrypi 4.1.13-v7+ #826 SMP PREEMPT Fri Nov 13 20:19:03 GMT 2015 armv7l

GNU/Linux

As of 2016-06-20, the latest version reports as follows (on a Pi Zero):

Linux pizero 4.4.11+ #888 Mon May 23 20:02:58 BST 2016 armv6l GNU/Linux

The steps involved are:

sudo apt-get update

sudo apt-get upgrade

To upgrade the distribution we would run:

sudo apt-get update

sudo apt-get dist-upgrade

Despite these instructions, my experience on upgrading Raspbian is simply "don't". When ever I have upgraded a Raspbian environment, various things either stop working or eventually either stop working or don't behave as expected.

My recommendation, as painful as it sounds, is to re-install a virgin image and re-customize it. To not lose data, I suggest using a brand new microSD card rather than re-image the existing one. Once you are sure that your newly installed Pi has *everything* you want from the old image, then you can obviously re-use the original card.

When we run the command "**uname -a**" we are also told the kernel level. For example:

Linux raspi 4.4.9-v7+ #884 SMP Fri May 6 17:28:59 BST 2016 armv7l GNU/Linux

Tells us that we are running 4.4.9.

The file system

The Raspbian file system is a standard Linux file system hosted on a micro SD card. This is a hierarchical filesystem comprised of files and directories. It supports all the normal Linux commands for file manipulation:

- **cp** - copy files

- **mv** – move files

- **rm** – remove files

- **ls** – list files

- **ln** – link files

- **mkdir** – make a directory

- **rmdir** – remove a directory

- **chmod** – change file and directory permissions

- **mount** – mount a file system for use.

- **umount** – un-mount a previously mounted file system.

File permissions

On a Linux OS, files and directories have permissions associated with them. By and large there are three permissions a file can have which are "read", "write" and "execute". These declare whether a file can be read, written to or be executed. A file also has the concept of an owner and a group.

When we talk about permissions, we further categorize the permissions into those that are allowed for the owner, those that are allowed for members of the group associated with the file and those that are allowed for everyone else (i.e. neither the owner nor a member of the group).

We thus end up with nine specific permissions:

• owner – read / write / execute

• group member – read / write / execute

• others – read / write / execute

An encoding scheme has been used for visualizing and describing permissions for files using the octal numbering system (base 8).
If we imagine that the three permissions were described in 3 bit binary with an order of read / write / execute then we would have permissions of "rwx" … or [1/0][1/0][1/0]. So, in binary, permissions of 101 would say we have permission to read and execute but not write. If we translate this binary into octal, it would be written as 4+0+1 = 5.
Thus we can represent a set of read / write / execute permissions as a single octal digit (0-7). Combining this with the notion that we have three sets of permissions (user, group and other), we can completely describe all the permissions on a file

with three octal digits. For example, 755 would be a value of 7 for user (read / write / execute) and 5 for both group and other (read / execute).

The Linux command called **chmod** can be used to set the permissions. For example:

chmod 755 myFile

Does this sound complicated? Yes it does … however it is how Unix has been handled since its inception. There are other mechanisms should you not wish to remember these encodings and those can be read about in the man pages for **chmod**.

Hardware interfacing:

Other than the extremely cheap price of the Pi, the one other attribute that stands out about it is its ability to interface with an arbitrary amount of hardware components through electronic connections.

In this section, we examine some of the core generic capabilities available to us to interface the Pi with a wide variety of hardware.

1. Pin mapping:

When we think of hardware pins, we immediately consider the notion that we can identify a pin by some common number.   For example, if I say "Pin 13", then you should be able to find "Pin 13" on the board.   The problem with the Pi is that there are multiple conventions for naming pins. Specifically, there are four families:

• Physical header numbering
• Broadcom pin numbering
• Broadcom GPIO numbering
• WiringPi numbering

To make matters even more complex, the hardware connectors on different models of the Pi differ from each other. There are basically two hardware connectors. One has 26 pins and the other has 40 pins.

As such, it is absolutely vital that when you think you are reading and writing from a pin, you have researched and understood the identification of that pin. Simply saying "Pin 13" is ambiguous without qualifying the pin identification technique that you are using.

(A fantastic source of pin-outs can be found at www.pighixxx.com. These show the mappings for all common pin numbering schemes.)

To make things easier now, here is an example of a Pi pin mapping with different families:

Raspberry Pi 2 Model B (J8 Header)

GPIO#	NAME		NAME	GPIO#
	3.3 VDC Power	A2	5.0 VDC Power	
8	GPIO 8 SDA1 (I2C)		5.0 VDC Power	
9	GPIO 9 SCL1 (I2C)		Ground	
7	GPIO 7 GPCLK0		GPIO 15 TxD (UART)	15
	Ground		GPIO 16 RxD (UART)	16
0	GPIO 0		GPIO 1 PCM_CLK/PWM0	1
2	GPIO 2		Ground	
3	GPIO 3		GPIO 4	4
	3.3 VDC Power		GPIO 5	5
12	GPIO 12 MOSI (SPI)		Ground	
13	GPIO 13 MISO (SPI)		GPIO 6	6
14	GPIO 14 SCLK (SPI)		GPIO 10 CE0 (SPI)	10
	Ground		GPIO 11 CE1 (SPI)	11
	SDA0 (I2C ID EEPROM)		SCL0 (I2C ID EEPROM)	
21	GPIO 21 GPCLK1		Ground	
22	GPIO 22 GPCLK2		GPIO 26 PWM0	26
23	GPIO 23 PWM1		Ground	
24	GPIO 24 PCM_FS/PWM1		GPIO 27	27
25	GPIO 25		GPIO 28 PCM_DIN	28
	Ground		GPIO 29 PCM_DOUT	29

And this is the table explaining the pinout:

Physical	Broadcom	GPIO	WiringPi / Pi4J	Special
2	03	GPIO 02	GPIO 08	SDA1
3	05	GPIO 03	GPIO 09	SCL1
4	07	GPIO 04	GPIO 07	GPCLK0
6	11	GPIO 17	GPIO 00	
7	13	GPIO 27	GPIO 02	
8	15	GPIO 22	GPIO 03	
10	19	GPIO 10	GPIO 12	MOSI
11	21	GPIO 09	GPIO 13	MISO
12	23	GPIO 11	GPIO 14	SCLK
15	29	GPIO 05	GPIO 21	GPCLK1
16	31	GPIO 06	GPIO 22	GPCLK2
17	33	GPIO 13	GPIO 23	PWM1
18	35	GPIO 19	GPIO 24	PCF_FS / PWM1
19	37	GPIO 26	GPIO 25	
21	40	GPIO 21	GPIO 29	PCM_DOUT
22	38	GPIO 20	GPIO 28	PCM_DIN
23	36	GPIO 16	GPIO 27	
25	32	GPIO 12	GPIO 26	PWM0
28	26	GPIO 07	GPIO 11	CE1
29	24	GPIO 08	GPIO 10	CE0
30	22	GPIO 25	GPIO 06	
32	18	GPIO 24	GPIO 05	
33	16	GPIO 23	GPIO 04	
35	12	GPIO 18	GPIO 01	PCM_CLK / PWM0
36	10	GPIO 15	GPIO 16	RxD
37	08	GPIO 14	GPIO 15	TxD

a. GPIO

GPIOs are the General Purpose Input/Outputs. They provide the primary mechanism to read and write electrical signals to and from the Pi.

The theory of General Purpose Input/Output (GPIO) is the simplest of all the hardware interfaces to understand. With GPIO a device exposes a set of physical pins. These pins can either be used to output an electrical signal for consumption by a second device connected to the pin or can be used to read the electrical signal present on a pin as set by a second device. At any one time, each pin can either be defined as an output pin or an input pin.

Obviously, it can't be both at the same time though may switch roles as needed. When a pin is flagged as output, it can source a current that can be consumed by a connected peripheral however care must be taken. GPIOs on MCUs are only able to source a small amount of current and trying to draw too much can irreparably damage the device. Take care to consult the appropriate data sheets for any devices connected to determine their current requirements and ensure that you are not asking for too much current from your MCU.

The Pi has GPIO available to it. There are a maximum of 26 pins available for this purpose. The signal levels on the Pi are 3V. What this means is the maximum output signal is 3V and the maximum input signal must also be 3V. Let us be very clear on this. If you attempt to apply an input signal higher than 3V you run a very distinct risk that you will damage or destroy your Pi. In addition, the maximum output current that may safely be drawn from an output GPIO pin is 3mA. Again, if you try and draw more current that this you risk the destruction of your Pi.

GPIO pins can be configured as input (meaning that we can read signal from them and they don't output signals) or they can be configured as output (meaning that we can write signals to them). On power-up, the majority of the pins are in input mode.

For input mode pins, we also have the notion of pull-up or pull-down resistors that are internal to the device. When we think of an input signal being applied to a pin, we usually consider it high or low … however there is a third possibility, namely that there is no signal applied to the pin. Think of a pin connected to a button and the button being open. In this scenario, what is the value of the pin should we read it? This is where the pull-up and pull-down resistors come into play. These are resistors that supply sufficient signal that if no alternate signal is supplied, a read of an open circuit pin will result in either a high (pull-up) or a low (pull-down).

Certain pins have overloaded functions and as such the Pi must be placed in a "mode" to designate how the pins are going to be used. For example, GPIO pins GPIO14 and GPIO15 can double as TXD and RXD for UART … but we can't use them as both GPIO and UART at the same time.

A number of libraries have been written to provide interfaces to the GPIO world from the Pi world. Such as:
• WiringPi
• Pigpio…

b. SPI:
SPI is a parallel to serial bi-directional protocol for

connecting a wide variety of devices.
SPI theory.

SPI is a serial protocol used to communicate
between masters and slaves. All slaves connect to
the same bus but only the slave with its SS (Ship
Select) driven pin low can transmit. SPI is a full
duplex protocol. What this means is that while data
is being pushed out from the master to the slave
over the MOSI line, the slave is simultaneously
sending data back to the master over the MISO line.

The MOSI pin contains the serial data from the
master to the slave while the MISO pin contains the
data from the slave to the master. The master and
slaves synchronize their transmissions using a
common clock signal.

A little diagram explaining is below:

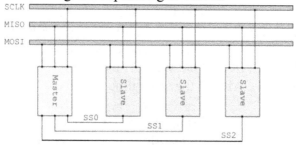

It is invalid for the master to drive more than one
slave select line low at any one time.
There three most important pins:
• MISO – Master In, Slave Out – Sending data to
the master from the slave
• MOSI – Master Out, Slave In – Sending data to

the slave from the master
• SCK (SCLK) – Serial Clock – Synchronizes data from the master/slave relationship
There is also an additional signal:
• SS (CSN (Chip Select NOT), NSS) – Slave Select – Used to enable/disable the slave so that there can be multiple slaves. SS low means slave is the active slave.
Since this is a serial protocol and we will receive data in bytes, we need to be cognizant of whether or not data will arrive LSB first or MSB first. There will be an option to control this.

For the clock, we will be latching data and we will need to know what edges and settings are important. There will be a clock mode option to control this. In SPI there are two attributes called phase and polarity. Phase (CPHA) is whether we are latching data on high or low and Polarity (CPOL) is whether high or low means that the clock is idle.

SPI on the Pi
The physical pins for SPI are 19 (MOSI), 21 (MISO), 23 (SCLK), 24 (CE0), 26 (CE1).

c. I2C:
The Inter-IC (I2C) protocol is a protocol for connecting multiple devices together that provides a way to transmit 8 bit bytes over a serial link. Originally developed by Phillips Semiconductors it is now part of NXP Semiconductors.
I2C theory: The I2C interface is a serial interface technology for accessing devices. The protocol is

also called the Two Wire Interface as it uses only two signal bus lines. These signal bus lines are called SDA (Data) and SCL (Clock). I2C allows for bidirectional communication. Attached to these lines are devices that wish to communicate.

One device holds a special role and is known as the bus master. It is the master that is the coordinator of all activities and is responsible for generating the clock. All other devices attached to the bus are known as slave devices.

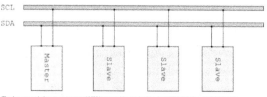

The data transmission rates are up to 100kbits/second in standard mode and 400kbits/second in fast mode.

Each slave device has a distinct and unique address upon the bus. It is the master that always initiates communication which may be either a send request to send data to a specific slave or a read request which asks the slave to respond with specific data.

Unless the master explicitly addresses a slave, it must keep silent. The device addresses are commonly 7 bits in size. The master sends the address of the device with which it wishes to communicate. Immediately following the address is a bit that indicates whether this is a read request (1) or a write request (0).

I2C on the Pi
The physical pins for I2C are fixed and physical pin 03 (SDA) and physical pin 05 (SCL).

d. PWM:
PWM theory: The idea behind pulse width modulation is that we can think of regular pulses of output signals as encoding information by how long the signal is kept high vs low.

Let us imagine that we have a period of 1Hz (one thing per second).

Now let us assume that we raise the output voltage to a level of high for ½ of a second at the start of the period. This would give us a square wave which starts high, lasts for 500 milliseconds and then drops low for the next 500 milliseconds. This repeats on into the future.

The duration that the pulse is high relative to the period allows us to encode an analog value onto digital signals. If the pulse is 100% high for the period then the encoded value would be 1.0. If the pulse is 100% low for the period, then the encoded value would be 0.0. If the pulse is on for "n" milliseconds (where n is less than 1000), then the encoded value would be n/1000.

Typically, the length of a period is not a whole second but much, much smaller allowing us to output many differing values very quickly. The amount of time that the signal is high relative to the period is called the "duty cycle". This encoding technique is called "Pulse Width Modulation" or "PWM".

There are a variety of purposes for PWM. Some are output data encoders. One commonly seen purpose is to control the brightness of an LED. If we apply maximum voltage to an LED, it is maximally bright. If we apply ½ the voltage, it is about ½ the brightness. By applying a fast period PWM signal to the input of an LED, the duty cycle becomes the brightness of the LED. The way this works is that either full voltage or no voltage is applied to the LED but because the period is so short, the "average" voltage over time follows the duty cycle and even though the LED is flickering on or off, it is so fast that our eyes can't detect it and all we see is the apparent brightness change.

PWM on the Pi
There are two hardware PWM output channels on the BCM283* chips identified as PWM0 and PWM1. On an old 26 pin header, only PWM0 is exposed. If we are willing to accept a little jitter, we can also use software PWM.

e. UART:
UART theory:
A UART is a mechanism to transmit and receive parallel data over a serial line connection. The data being transmitted is serialized into a sequence of bits and sent down the wire. The receiver receives the bits and assembles them back into the original

data. Both the sender and receiver pre-agree on the transmission rate of the data. This is called the baud rate. Before data is transmitted, a start bit is flagged on the wire to indicate that data is about to follow.

Then comes the 8 bits of data followed by a single stop bit. It is the start bit that allows the sender and receiver to synchronize on their clocks for the remaining bits. The idle state of a serial line is high. There is also the option of supplying parity bits and other control information. Some baud rates that are common are 9600, 19200, 57600 and 115200.

Remember that these are bit transmission rates and not byte rates. Since a single byte will have at least two additional bits (start and stop), this means that there are 10 bits to be transmitted for each byte. As such, a baud rate of 9600 may mean 960 (9600 / 10) bytes per second as opposed to 1200 (9600 / 8) bytes per second.

UART on the Pi
The Pi has a UART interface with TX and RX pins. The pins are located at physical locations 8 (TXD) and 10 (RXD).
USB:
The nature of USB devices can be found with the lsusb command. From there, you can add the -v (verbose) option and filter with the -s devNum option.
For example, here is an output from **lssub**:

Bus 001 Device 005: ID 18ec:3399 Arkmicro
Technologies Inc.
Bus 001 Device 007: ID 0bda:8172 Realtek
Semiconductor Corp. RTL8191SU 802.11n LAN
Adapter
Bus 001 Device 004: ID 0bda:8176 Realtek
Semiconductor Corp. RTL8188CUS 802.11n
WLAN
Adapter
Bus 001 Device 003: ID 0424:ec00 Standard
Microsystems Corp. SMSC9512/9514 Fast
Ethernet Adapter
Bus 001 Device 002: ID 0424:9514 Standard
Microsystems Corp.
Bus 001 Device 001: ID 1d6b:0002 Linux
Foundation 2.0 root hub

When we look at the output of a USB listing, we
sometimes see pairs of numbers. In the above, we
can see 18ec:3399 and 0bda:8172.

The first of these numbers is called a vendor id and
each product vendor has been allocated a unique
code. The second number is a product id and
corresponds to a product registered by that vendor.
When a USB device connects to a computer, the
computer can query these codes and learn what kind
of device it is that has attached.

2. Audio:

The Pi is capable of generating an audio output signal. There are two possible output destinations. The first is to carry the audio signal as part of the HDMI output. The other is to carry it through the 3.5mm output jack (Note: The Pi Zero does not have a 3.5mm jack).

Only one of these outputs can be used at one time. The default is to attempt to auto-sense the type to be used. This is accomplished by the HDMI driver interrogating the HDMI signals which should query the other end of the HDMI cable typically connected to your TV. If the HDMI signal states that it is capable of handling audio, then HDMI will be used as the audio output, otherwise the 3.5mm jack will be used.

3. Ethernet:

All the Pi models with the exception of the Pi Zero come with an Ethernet socket (RJ45) and associated controller logic. For a few dollars, one can buy a USB to Ethernet adapter to attach to a Pi Zero.

4. Video output

All the Pis have the ability to output HDMI quality video signals. Note that the Pi Zero has a smaller HDMI connector than the other Pis and an adapter is normally required. In addition, RCA composite video can also be externalized. On the Pi Zero, there is no supplied connection but there is the ability to wire an RCA connector. On the top of the board there are some solderable holes into which wires can be connected that can join to the RCA connector that can then be plugged into a TV. If the Pi Zero is booted without an HDMI connector, the RCA output will be used.

5. Camera

Through USB, many USB attachable webcams can be used. However, the Pi has special hardware support for a dedicated camera module. This is a 5 megapixel device that is attached through a ribbon cable onto a dedicated socket on the Pi board itself.

The camera is capable of recording at 1080p video speeds (1920x1080) at 30 frames per second using the H.264 encoding scheme. It needs special applications in order to access it. These include Raspivid for video capture and Raspistill for still image capture.

Programming for beginners

One of the exciting aspects of the Pi environment is that one is not forced to work in any particular programming language when building Pi applications. One has a wealth of choices available. Languages available include C, C++, Java, JavaScript, Python, C# and more. Some are much more commonly used and prevalent than others and for some languages we even have multiple choices of compiler and environment to use. With choice comes decision.

When you wish to undertake a project, which language do you use? Despite what many folks might argue, my vote is to use the one you "want" to use (where possible). The choice of one language over another can quickly break down into a religious battle where personal bias holds as much argument as technical merits.

1. Python programming

Python is a good general purpose language that is mature and stable. It offers many of the features we expect to find in other languages such as objects, procedural programming and more. Similar to Java, the Python language is distributed with a large set of pre-supplied extension modules that are themselves written in Python. As such, not only should one be studying the Python language but also the existence of the various modules. It may be that Python is already installed on your Pi. At the shell enter:

$ python -V

There are a variety of different python versions out there including 2.6, 2.7, 3.0 and 3.4.

We can run python just by entering the command "python". Running it with the "-h" flag lists us the command options available to us. The most common way to invoke a Python application is to place it in a file and run:

$ python <fileName>

however, running python by itself puts us into an interactive interpreter.

Python is a cross between an interpreted language and a compiled language. When we run a python program it is compiled then and there and then executed. For modules, the compilation output is saved.

If one wants to write a shell script that contains Python, we can being the script with:

#!/usr/bin/python

A more common form is to start the script with

#!/usr/bin/env python

This will run the "python" command found in the PATH environment variable.

In C and Java, we can group multiple statements together with curly braces. For example:

if (expression) {

statement1;

statement2;

statement3;

}

The statements between the braces are a grouping of statements. In Python, the designers have chosen to use indentation to signify grouping.

if (expression)

    statement1;

    statement2;

    statement3;

statement4;

In the above, statements 1,2 and 3 are executed if the expression is true. Statement 4 falls outside the grouping and will always be executed. If you are familiar with other languages, this is a significant difference.

Python provides some interesting data structures:

• A list – [1, 3.141, "elephant"]

• A tuple – (1,2,3)

• A dictionary - {'lng': 35.123, 'lat': -97.45}

Every variable in Python is an object with the special object called "None" referring to null.

With expressions we have boolean values called

True and False.

Variables do not have to be declared prior to use. The act of assigning a value to a variable causes it to be created.

Objects can have attributes associated with them. We refer to an attribute of an object using the "." operator. For example x.y refers to the attribute called y of the object called x.

When working on the Pi, we commonly wish to manipulate bits of data and we have bitwise operations including:

Operator Description

~ Bitwise inversion (not X)

<< Left bit shift

>> Right bit shift

& Bitwise AND

| Bitwise OR

^ Bitwise Excluisve OR (XOR)

The core language constructs are also present:

if <expression>:

statement1

statement2

elif <expression>:

statement3

else:

statement4

while <expression>:

statement1

statement2

for <var> in <iterable>:

statement1

statement2

The special function range() can be used to produce iterables. For example:

- **range(x)** – produces [0, 1, 2, … , x-1]

- **range(x,y)** – produces [x, x+1, x+2, …, y-1]

Functions can be defined using the def keyword:

def <functionName>(parameters):

statement1

statement2

Variables defined in a function are local in name scope to that function. To access the global variable, we need to

define that we wish to do such with **global <variableName>.**

Object oriented classes can be defined with:

class <className>(<baseClass>):

   statement1

   statement2

methods defined in classes always have a first parameter that by convention is called self.

Variables which are private to a class should start with two underscores.

Instances of classes are created by invoking the class name. For example:

class C:

   statement1

   statement2

myInstance = C()

If a function called __init__ is defined in the class then this is invoked as the constructor.

We can import modules using the import statement:

import <ModuleName>

If you are going to be doing Python development, you must install the package called **python-dev**:

$ sudo apt-get install python-dev

1. C programming

To be honest, we are not going to get far in the tasks we are looking to achieve without some skills in C programming and knowledge of the associated development tools. C is one step up from writing assembly language programs, however it is a big step up which is goodness. C provides us a useful mix between high level programming with concepts such as named variables, looping structures, scopes, function calls and more while at the same time providing us all the capabilities we need to "twiddle" bits and bytes at arbitrary memory locations.

Since Linux (and hence Raspbian) are themselves predominantly written in C, the linkage between our own custom applications and the operating system is very close. Also, should we get into writing "bare metal" applications, C and assembler are our primary choices.

C Programming theory

We'll start with the basics. We use an editor to enter source C code. We save the source to files giving them names ending in ".c" which is by unanimous convention, the file type for a C language program. Since the C source code is not directly executable, we must compile that source into machine instructions the Pi can understand. We use a tool called a C compiler to perform that task. The Raspbian environment provides the popular GNU C Compiler (GCC) to perform that task. The result of compilation is a new file with a file suffix of ".o". This is what is called a relocatable object file. The nature of this is that it contains compiled code but that code is not yet ready to run.

The addresses that are used for memory reads and writes as well as branch locations have not yet been fixed. Our next step is to perform a step called "linking" which takes one or more object files plus libraries and link edits them together which results in the final executable. Think of this like putting the pieces of a jigsaw puzzle together. This executable has had its addresses resolved and is ready to be run. The linking can again be performed with the same C compiler. The overall flow is as follows:

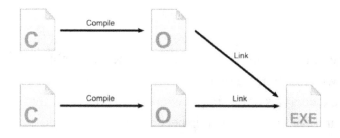

The primary value of going through this multi-step process is that we can break our large programs into multiple source files each of which results in its own object file. We can then link these object files together to produce our desired executable. The benefit of this is that if we change just one source file, we only have to recompile the single source file that changed to build its new object file.

When we link edit the new object file with the already existing object files from previous compiles, we end up with our new executable. This can save considerable time for very large applications as we don't have to continually recompile all our code for each small change.

A second and equally important reason for this process is that we can take object files and group them together by adding them to an archive file. An archive file typically starts with **"lib"** and ends with the file suffix of **".a"**.

When we are linking our application, we now no longer need to name each of the object files but instead supply the archive file. The linker is intelligent enough to know which of the object files within the archive are needed for the executable and which can be ignored. This means that our resulting executables don't simply contain everything in the archive but only what is needed for execution.

This library mechanism serves another purpose that is possibly the secret sauce that makes everything work well.

By placing object files in an archive, we can distribute that archive to other programmers and they can make calls to functions that are contained within the object files within the archive without having to know exactly what is contained within the archive or how they work. This provides the powerful concept of reusable code. If I were to write a set of new C functions of high quality and value, I could packed them up in a library and supply only the library and documentation. You could then use those functions merely by linking with the library.

The Linux operating system itself provides a huge array of functions contained within libraries supplied by the operating system.

The C compiler does double duty when it comes time to perform the linking. When it is executed with different inputs, it performs the linking. To be clear, the C compiler is capable of both compiling a source file to an object file and is also capable of linking together object files with optional libraries to produce an executable.

If your program should consist of only a few C source files, you can combine these steps into one command which both compiles and links the application in one single step. This, however, is not a common circumstance. Instead what we usually wish to do is compile only the source files that have changed and then link everything together.

The C compiler will compile a source file to an object file when asked but it has no deeper intelligence to know about which files have changed or not changed. To efficiently compile applications together, such that only the changed source files are re-compiled, we need a tool which can detect changes to source files and re-compile only those that need re-compilation.

Fortunately, a tool called **"make"** is provided to perform exactly that task. The way **make** works is that we provide it a set of rules that it should follow to build an executable. To build an executable, we tell it the names of the object files that it should link together. For each object file, we tell it the corresponding name of the source file that needs to be compiled to produce that object file. If we think this through for a while, we will see that to build an executable, we depend on the existence of a set of object files and those object files depend on the C source files. An object file is considered out of date if the source file has a time stamp of when it was last changed which is newer than the time stamp of when the object file was created. In addition, an executable is considered out of date if the file containing that executable has a time stamp older than any of the resulting object files.

This chain of thinking and examination of source file, object file and executable file time stamps is what is handled through the **make** tool. Since **make** doesn't know by itself which files constitute our project, we must provide those instructions in a separate file which is called a Makefile.

This Makefile contains the rules that make follows when executed. Each rule commonly takes two inputs. The target file we wish to create and the set of one or more files that are the dependencies to create that target. So if an executable is our target, its dependencies will be the set of object files and each object file will itself be a separate target which has the C source file as its dependency.

When we ask make to build our executable, it works through the instructions contained within the Makefile to determine which targets are out of date.

For each rule that detects that a target is out of date, a Raspbian command is supplied that is responsible for creating the target from the corresponding dependency files.

For example, if make determines that an object file is out of date with respect to its corresponding source file, the command would be a request to compile the source to produce the new object. If an executable is out of date with respect to its object files, the command would be a request to link together the object files.

C tools for Pi

GNU C is the common C compiler environment. To determine the level of C installed, run **gcc -v** and look for the version indicator. For example, on my current Raspbian, the output ends with:

gcc version 4.9.2 (Raspbian 4.9.2-10)

Simple compilation

To compile and run a program on the Pi we can use the gcc compiler. For example, let us look at the following simple C program:

nano hello.c   (to create a C file named hello.c and to write in it**)**

(Then copy the following code into)

```c
#include<stdio.h>

main()

{

    printf("Hello World");

}
```

(type ctrl+x then Y and   ENTER to exit and save)

If we then compile the program with:

gcc hello.c

we will find that we have an executable called **a.out**. If we run this with **./a.out**, we will see the message printed for us.

Distance access to RPI

The story of networking on a Linux platform is deep and wide. Here are some of the key facts that will be necessary for you to learn.

To determine the Pi's IP address, use the command **ifconfig** which lists all the network interfaces known to Linux.

If your PC is a windows PC, get, install and learn the PuTTY tool. PuTTY provides a remote terminal client that includes both Telnet and SSH support. See here: http://www.putty.org/

Networking Devices

Depending on the model of Pi you are using you may or may not have an Ethernet port. If you don't, then you will likely be adding a WiFi USB dongle. In fact, even if you do have an Ethernet port, it is still likely you will be adding a dongle. Let us now look at some of the considerations when using these physical interfaces.

1. Ethernet

If your Pi has an Ethernet port then it is based on the LAN9512 chip set with a 10/100Mb capacity.

• Setting up a static Ethernet IP Address

There are many times that I find myself on the road with only a Pi and a laptop. As such, I have no WiFi nor HDMI video (TV). To be productive, I plug a regular Ethernet cable into my Pi and the other end into my laptop. My laptop has a static IP address for its end of the Ethernet at 192.168.2.2 and I want my Pi to also have a static IP address of 192.168.2.3. When set up in that fashion, I can then reach one from the other. However, running the **ifconfig** command at the console may not be an option so I needed to find a way to configure such that the Ethernet static IP address was present at boot. The solution is quite simple. We edit the file called **/etc/dhcpcd.conf** and add the following lines at the end:

 # Static IP configuration

interface eth0

static ip_address=192.168.3.2/24

Following a restart, the Pi is ready to be connected.

• Using Windows Internet Connection Sharing

Imagine you are in a hotel room and you have your Windows laptop PC which is connected to the hotel WiFi. You now connect your Pi to the laptop via

Ethernet and you can SSH into the Pi. Great. You then realize that you want to connect to the Internet from the Pi … but … huh … it doesn't work. That is correct … if we follow the story, the Windows PC is connected to the Internet and the Pi is connected to the PC but that doesn't mean that the Pi is connected to the Internet. A few new things have to happen. First of all, we need to enable "Internet Connection Sharing" on the WiFi adapter and name the Ethernet adapter as the connection to be shared. Next, on the Pi, we need to add a default route statement that will send all traffic not on the Pi's local LAN to the Ethernet adapter on the PC which will THEN be routed to the Internet. Assuming that the PC's Ethernet address is 192.168.2.2, then on the Pi we would run:

$ sudo route add -net default gw 192.168.2.2

We can check that this has taken effect by running:

$ route

Kernel IP routing table

Destination	Gateway	Genmask	Flags	Metric	Ref	Use Iface
default	192.168.2.2	0.0.0.0	UG	0	0	0 eth0
192.168.2.0	*	255.255.255.0	U	202	0	0 eth0

We see that the default gateway is now 192.168.2.2.

Finally, we need to edit **/etc/resolv.conf** to add

some default nameservers:

Google IPv4 nameservers

nameserver 8.8.8.8

nameserver 8.8.4.4

And that should be it … we can test by pinging some hostnames from the Pi which should now resolve. Note that if we are using DHCP client or some other networking components, the **resolv.conf** can be generated for us and will undo any hand editing we may have made. As an alternative, consider editing **dhcpcd.conf** and adding:

interface eth0

static ip_address=192.168.2.3/24

static domain_name_servers=8.8.8.8 8.8.4.4

The "static domain_name_servers" adds the entries we need.

2. WiFi

Some of the more common WiFi dongles out in the market are based on the Realtek 8192cu chip. We can configure some of the lower level properties of the device driver for this chip by editing the file called **/etc/modprobe.d/8192cu.conf**. When these chips power up, they may have a power saving mode associated with them. What that means is that after a period of no network activity, they can suspend themselves. In principle, this sounds great, but in practice, it can be a pain. We find that network applications such as NFS start to hang when accessed as the network to the Pi has been put to sleep and can take time to come back on-line. It is not uncommon for us to want to suspend the power suspension capabilities of the device. To do that, we can edit or create the **8192cu.conf** file in the directory **/etc/modprobe.d** and add the following:

options 8192cu rtw_power_mgnt=0 rtw_enusbss=0 rtw_ips_mode=1

After adding and rebooting, the device will no longer suspend itself. To see the current values of the device configuration, examine the files at **/sys/module/8192cu/*.** The ones in the **parameters** sub-folder are especially useful.

The command **iwconfig** can be used to display and change a variety of parameters associated with WiFi devices. Running **iwconfig** by itself produces a good summary of the qualities of the attached WiFi devices:

$ iwconfig

**wlan0 IEEE 802.11bgn ESSID:"kolban"
Nickname:"<WIFI@REALTEK>"**

**Mode:Managed Frequency:2.442 GHz Access
Point: A4:2B:8C:81:47:95**

Bit Rate:72.2 Mb/s Sensitivity:0/0

Retry:off RTS thr:off Fragment thr:off

Power Management:off

**Link Quality=100/100 Signal level=98/100 Noise
level=0/100**

**Rx invalid nwid:0 Rx invalid crypt:0 Rx invalid
frag:0**

**Tx excessive retries:0 Invalid misc:0 Missed
beacon:0**

lo no wireless extensions.

eth0 no wireless extensions.

3. Windows Laptop As Monitor for Raspberry Pi

To access your desktop interface of raspberry through your PC, you must follow the following steps:

a. Download and install required software in your PC :

PUTTY
(http://www.chiark.greenend.org.uk/~sgtatham/putty...)

VNC Viewer
(https://www.realvnc.com/download/viewer/)

b. Create SSH connection with your PI
- Open Putty software

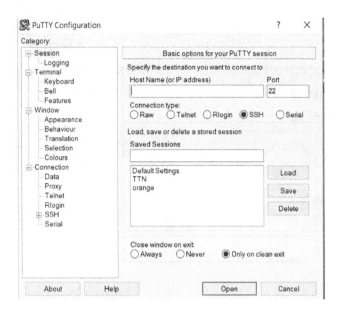

- Type in the **ip address** of raspberry pi (192.168.1.100) and click on open
- Type in "**pi**" as username and "**raspberry**" as password.
- Type in the command - "**sudo apt-get install tightvncserver**"
- When installation is completed again type "**tightvncserver**" and return.
- It will ask for a password. **Give the password** and give it again to **verify**
- Note down the **desktop number**. Here it is 1

c. Use VNC Viewer to View Pi Screen in Your Windows Laptop

- Open **VNC Viewer** software.

- Type in the IP address of raspberry pi with the desktop number like this - **192.168.1.100:1**
- Click on **connect**. If any security warning comes **ignore that and continue**. This is not harmful, so relax.
- .After that, the app will ask that password which you have given in the last step. **Give that and continue.**
- Now you are on the monitor of your raspberry pi.

Simple beginner Raspberry Pi project

Step 1: Things You Will Need

You will need the following components other than Raspberry Pi setup:

- 3*5mm led (X1)
- 3*100Ω Resistor (X1)
- Jumper wires
- Breadboard

Step 3: Setup Your Pi & The One Outline

Once you have the Raspberry Pi's case, power up the Raspberry Pi, connect the keyboard and the HDMI monitor.

Next, connect the Pi and the breadboard circuit as shown in the following diagram.

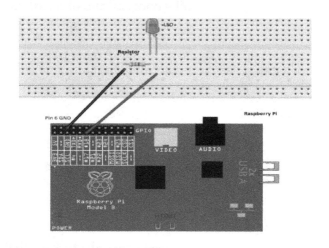

FIRST RASPBERRY PI PROJECT

Raspberry Pi B+ J8 Header

Pin#	NAME			NAME	Pin#
01	3.3v DC Power			DC Power 5v	02
03	GPIO02 (SDA1 , I2C)			DC Power 5v	04
05	GPIO03 (SCL1 , I2C)			Ground	06
07	GPIO04 (GPIO_GCLK)			(TXD0) GPIO14	08
09	Ground			(RXD0) GPIO15	10
11	GPIO17 (GPIO_GEN0)			(GPIO_GEN1) GPIO18	12
13	GPIO27 (GPIO_GEN2)			Ground	14
15	GPIO22 (GPIO_GEN3)			(GPIO_GEN4) GPIO23	16
17	3.3v DC Power			(GPIO_GEN5) GPIO24	18
19	GPIO10 (SPI_MOSI)			Ground	20
21	GPIO09 (SPI_MISO)			(GPIO_GEN6) GPIO25	22
23	GPIO11 (SPI_CLK)			(SPI_CE0_N) GPIO08	24
25	Ground			(SPI_CE1_N) GPIO07	26
27	ID_SD (I2C ID EEPROM)			(I2C ID EEPROM) ID_SC	28
29	GPIO05			Ground	30
31	GPIO06			GPIO12	32
33	GPIO13			Ground	34
35	GPIO19			GPIO16	36
37	GPIO26			GPIO20	38
39	Ground			GPIO21	40

Rev. 1.1
16/07/2014
http://www.element14.com